Wise D

Ruth Craft

Pictures by Nicola Smee

Collins

First published 1986 by William Collins Sons & Co Ltd, London and Glasgow
© text Ruth Craft 1986, © illustrations Nicola Smee 1986

It was breakfast time.
Vernon's mother was late for work.
Vernon was late for school.

"This is not the place for your sandwich box!" said Vernon's mother. She took the sandwich box off the top of the television.

"This is not the place for your handbag!" said Vernon. He took the handbag off the top of the kitchen bin.

Vernon and his mother were cross
with each other.

Their dog Rumble looked at them.
He was a wise dog.
He hid under the table.

Vernon's mother was frying eggs.

Vernon did not like eggs.
He looked at Rumble under the table.

Rumble sniffed.
He could smell the eggs.
Rumble stayed under
the table.
He was a wise dog.

Vernon drank his milk.

He ate lots of bread.

He ate a banana.

He did not eat his eggs.

Rumble licked his chops.
He was a wise dog.
He stayed under the table.

Vernon's plate was empty.
"Good boy, Vernon," said his mother.

Vernon and his mother were ready to go.

"I must give Rumble a biscuit.
  He is a good dog," said Vernon's mother.
"No," said Vernon. "He is too fat."

Vernon went out of the door and down
the path.

Vernon's mother thought,
"Poor Rumble."
She found a biscuit.
Rumble watched her.

Vernon's mother gave Rumble a cuddle.
She gave him a biscuit.

Vernon and his mother walked down
the road.
They were not cross with each other now.

Rumble stayed under the table.
He licked his chops.
He was a wise dog.